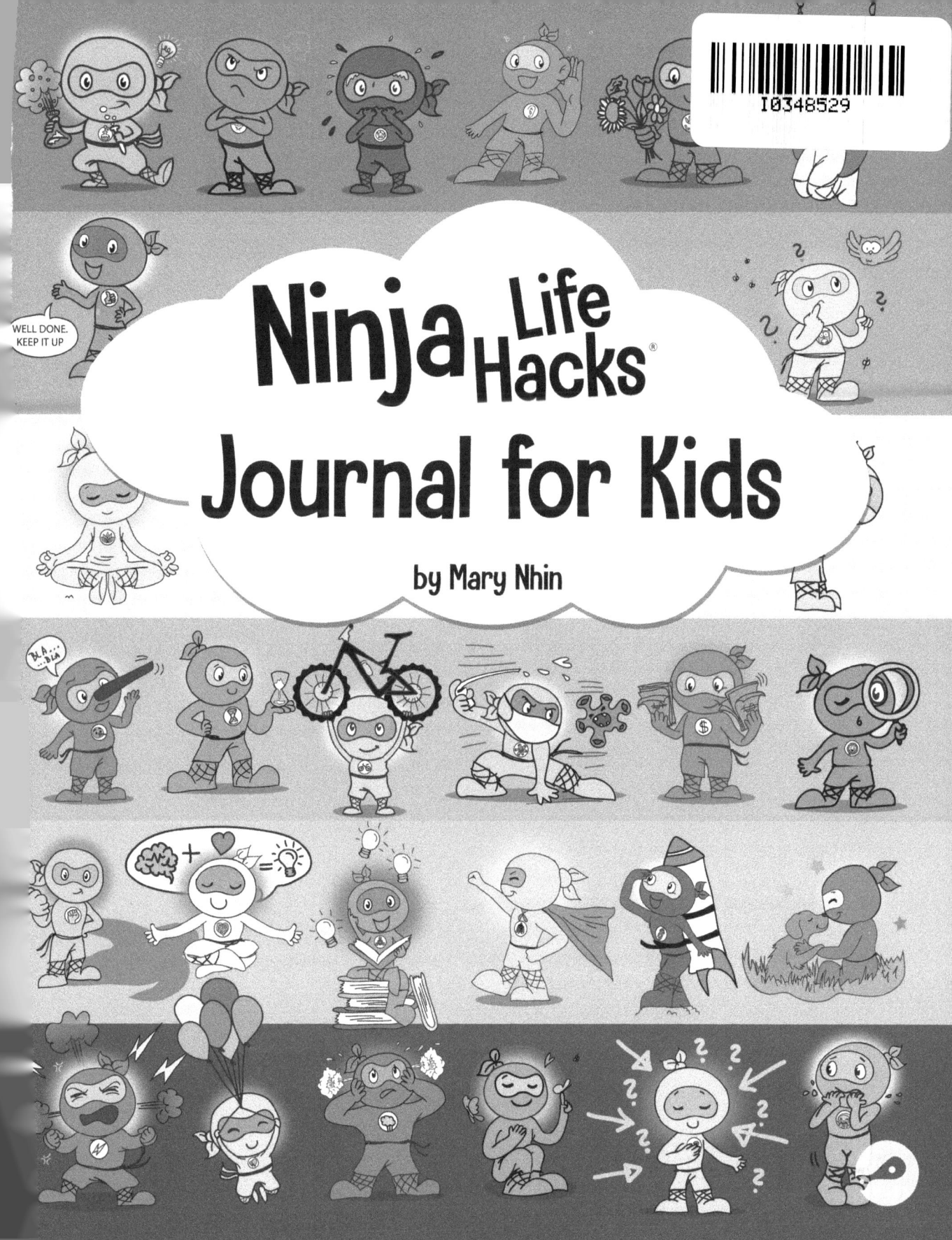

This book is dedicated to my children- Mikey, Kobe, and Jojo.

Copyright © 2023 by Grow Grit Press LLC. All rights reserved. No Chapter of this book may be reproduced in any form without permission in writing from the publisher. Please send bulk order requests to orders@ninjalifehacks.tv

Paperback ISBN: 978-1-63731-847-8
Hardcover ISBN: 978-1-63731-848-5

Printed and bound in the USA.
NinjaLifeHacks.tv

 # This Journal Belongs to:

_____

My Journal Partner is:

_____

What is the Ninja Life Hacks Journal?

This journal allows you to practice the ninja life hacks presented in our books. By practicing the methods and techniques, it will help you develop:

- ➡ Compassion
- ➡ Gratitude
- ➡ Positivity
- ➡ Honesty
- ➡ Growth mindset
- ➡ Fiscal fitness
- ➡ Courage
- ➡ Patience
- ➡ Grit
- ➡ Empathy
- ➡ Organizational skills
- ➡ Kindness
- ➡ Decision-making skills
- ➡ Humor
- ➡ Hope
- ➡ Communication skills
- ➡ Inclusion
- ➡ Diversity
- ➡ Focus

How do you use the Ninja Life Hacks Journal?

 Pick a time each day to write in your journal.

 Find a journal partner.

 Read the stories in the Ninja Life Hacks books series.

Table of Contents

Intro: About Me

1. Grit and Mental Toughness
2. Self-Care and Self-Love
3. Gratitude
4. Kindness
5. Positivity
6. Unplugged
7. Emotions
8. Environmentalism
9. Honesty

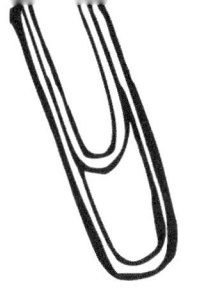

10. Growth Mindset
11. Money
12. Patience
13. Diversity
14. Courage
15. Organization
16. Calm
17. Effort
18. Confidence
19. Focus
20. Inclusion
21. Communication
22. Hope
23. Humor

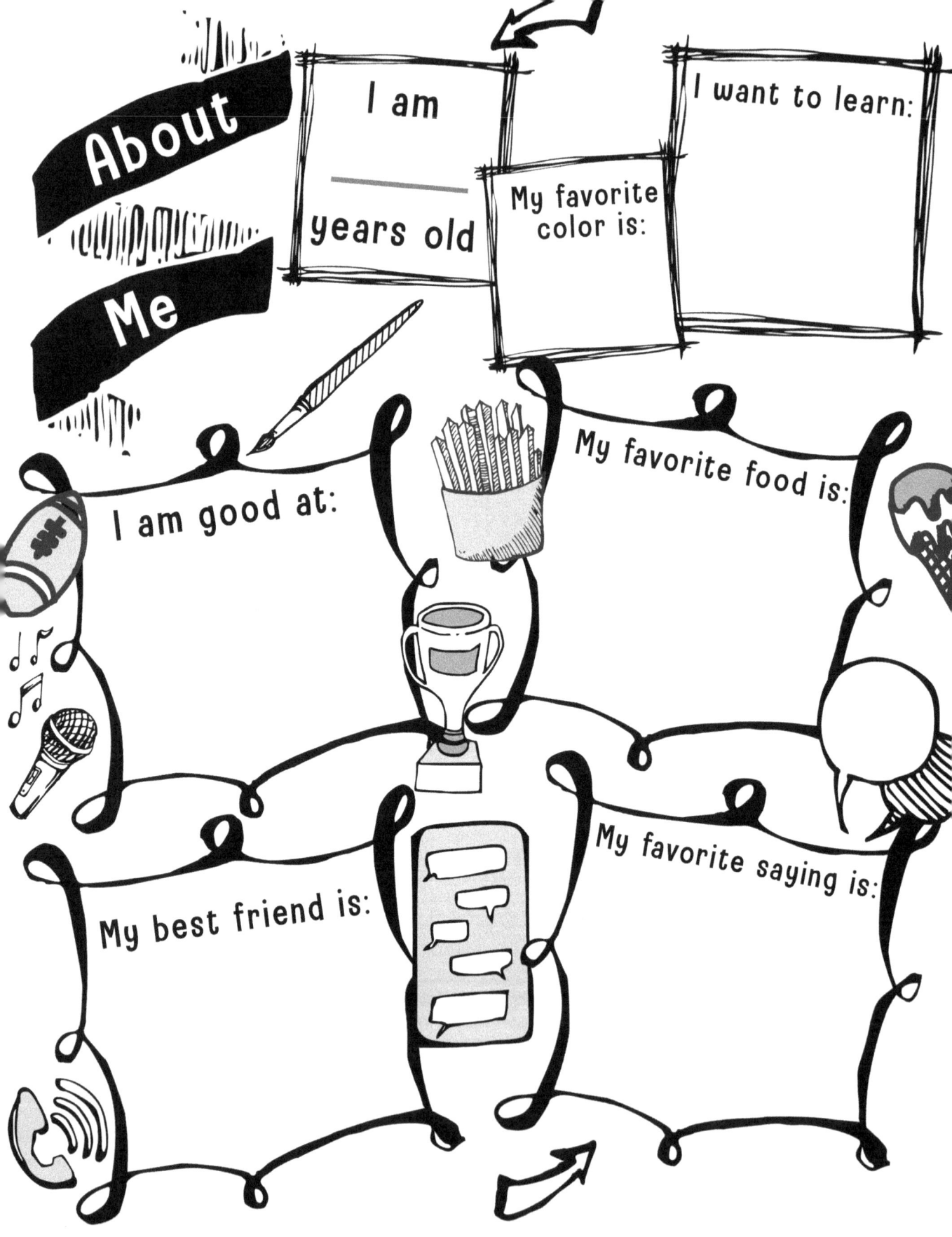

This is what makes me unique:

Circle the sentences that describe you.
Underline those that you would like to be.

I am kind.

I am confident.

I am grateful.

I am focused.

I am wise

I am organized.

I communicate well.

I am inclusive.

I am hopeful.

I am funny.

I am compassionate.

I am calm.

I am courageous.

I am positive.

I am gritty.

I care for the earth.

I am mentally tough.

Challenges help me grow.

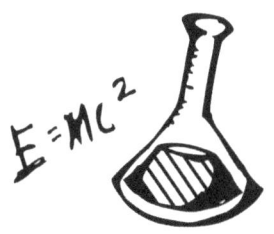

Grit and Mental Toughness

Chapter 1

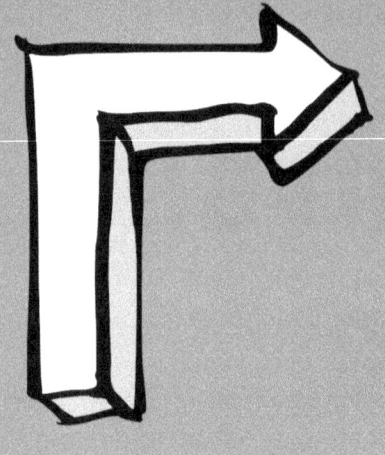

The mind is stronger than the body.

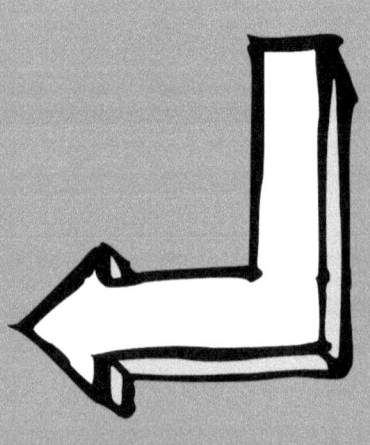

List or draw four things that you continued to try even though they were hard.

Having mental toughness allows us to overcome obstacles. When the going gets tough, grit allows us to not give up and focus until we reach our goals. How do you develop grit?

There are 4 tools that allow you to grow your grit. The grit strategy is called the 4 Cs:

4 Cs	Tool
Capable	Goals
Calm	Positive Mantras
Carefree	Minimizing
Confident	Visualization

Example	Your Example
I will practice 30 minutes a day, 4 times a week.	List your goals and how you will achieve them.
I can do this!	List your mantra here:
What's the worst thing that can happen?	Answer the question.
I am confident when I visualize my success.	Now close your eyes and visualize your success.

Self-Care and Self-Love

♡♡♡

Chapter 2

We can't pour from an empty cup.

List or draw five things that always bring a smile to your face.

What are some worries or fears you can let go of today?

Go outside and squint at the sun.

 Close your eyes.

Take ten deep breaths.

Gratitude

Chapter 3

Happy people are those who are grateful.

Gratitude walk and Scavenger Hunt

Go on a nature walk and marvel at Earth's bounties. Look around and take in all that you are grateful for. Then, draw or list them here:

Color in the things you are grateful for about yourself:

- ♥ My health, so I can swim and climb a mountain.
- ♥ My arms, so I can stretch.
- ♥ My legs, so I can run.
- ♥ My teeth, so I can chew food.
- ♥ My ears, so I can hear.
- ♥ My skin, so I can feel.
- ♥ My heart, so I can live.

Kindness

Chapter 4

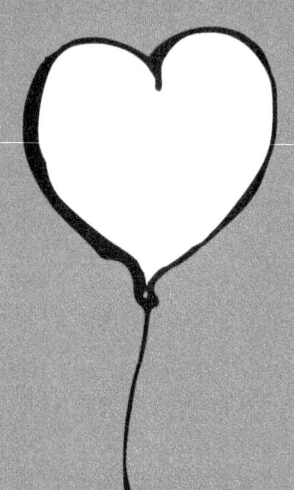

It costs

nothing

to be

kind.

Color in where you fall on this scale:

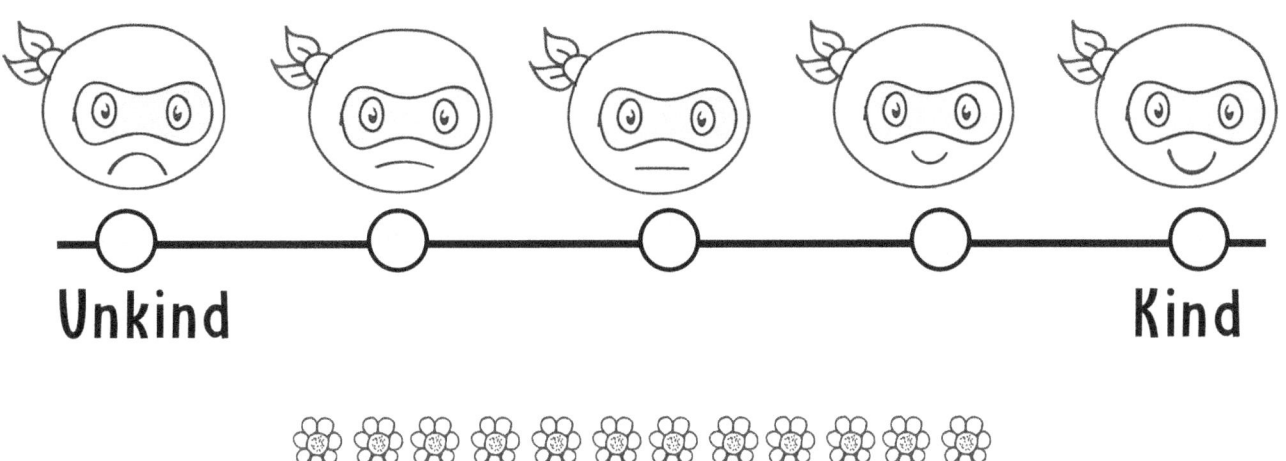

Unkind   Kind

Write down one kind thing you did for someone else in the past twenty-four hours.

Kind Ninja loves being caring and compassionate. But it was not always like this. It used to be more about "me, me, me.". Until one day, his heart changed.

Here are some things he did to change things around and be more kind to everyone and everything around him:

Pick up trash.
Help with chores.
Water the plants.
Help the elderly.
Take out the trash.
Say thank you and please more.

What are some things you can do to practice kindness? List or draw them here.

Positivity

Chapter 5

Be the **energy** you want to **attract.**

How do you change these negative thoughts to positive ones?

I can't do that.

_____

I'm not good at this.

_____

I don't think I'll be good.

_____

I'm not doing this right.

_____

What *positive* words can you say to yourself?

Place your hand down below and use your other hand to trace it's outline.

Write "I believe I am" in the center of the outline, then write a positive word that describes you on each finger!

Unplugged

Chapter 6

It's bad for your
brain
NOT
to
unplug.

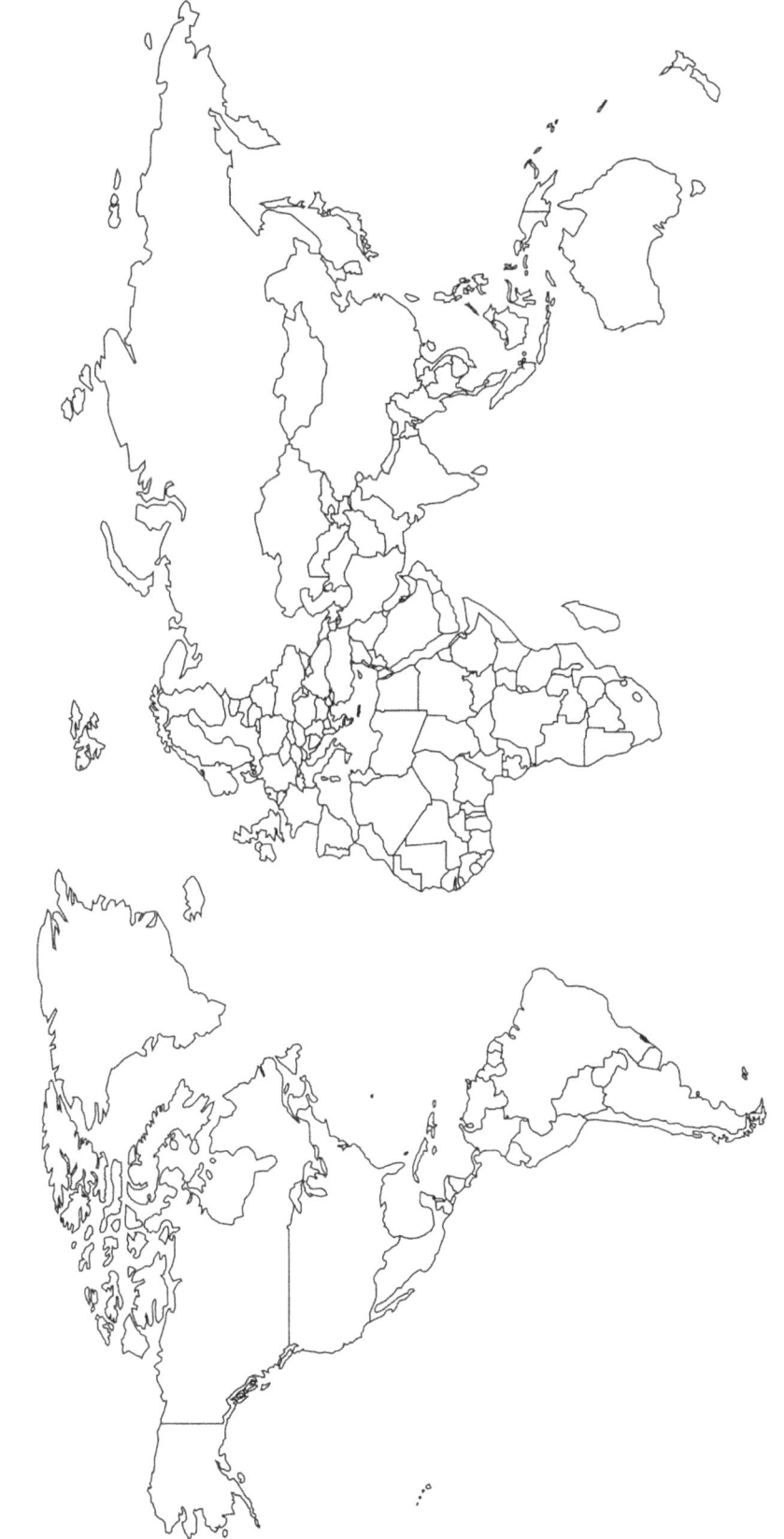

Unplugged Ninja was the calmest, coolest ninja around. But she wasn't always so calm, cool, and collected. She used to suffer from a bit of screen attachment.

Do you know the strategy she used to turn things around:

Fill in the blank with the 3 Rs:

_____ with something creative or active.

_____ with nature.

_____ with music or a book.

What would you do to unplug? List or draw them here:

Emotions

Chapter 7

Control your emotions, *DON'T* let them control you.

Things that make me happy	Things that make me mad	Things that make me anxious

What are 5 worries you could live without? Imagine yourself blowing them away once you've written them down.

Color in this spectrum with all the emotions you have experienced.

Anger	anxiety	STRESS
Positivity	LOVE	grumpy
JOY	shy	CALM
fear	HOPE	Compassion
Grateful	sadness	BRAVE
shame	Irritation	lazy

Environmentalism

Chapter 8

What we save, saves us.

Go outside and step on the grass with your bare feet. How does it feel?

How many living things can you find? List or draw them here.

Earth Ninja shows us how one little ninja can make a difference in the world by practicing three simple life habits:

Reduce
Reuse
Recycle

Circle the items in your house you can reuse, recycle, or reduce.

Honesty

Chapter 9

Honesty
is the
best
policy.

-Benjamin Franklin

When was a time you could've lied but you chose not to?

Dishonest Ninja didn't think he was hurting anyone when he chose not to tell the truth.

But what he didn't understand was that each time he lied, he was hurting someone. Because when he told a lie, it changed HIM just a little bit each time.

He changed when he realized that lying made him feel bad inside. It ultimately hurt him by making him feel anxious, worried, and afraid.

Where do you fall on the honesty spectrum?
Put an **X** where you are now and
an **O** where you want to be.

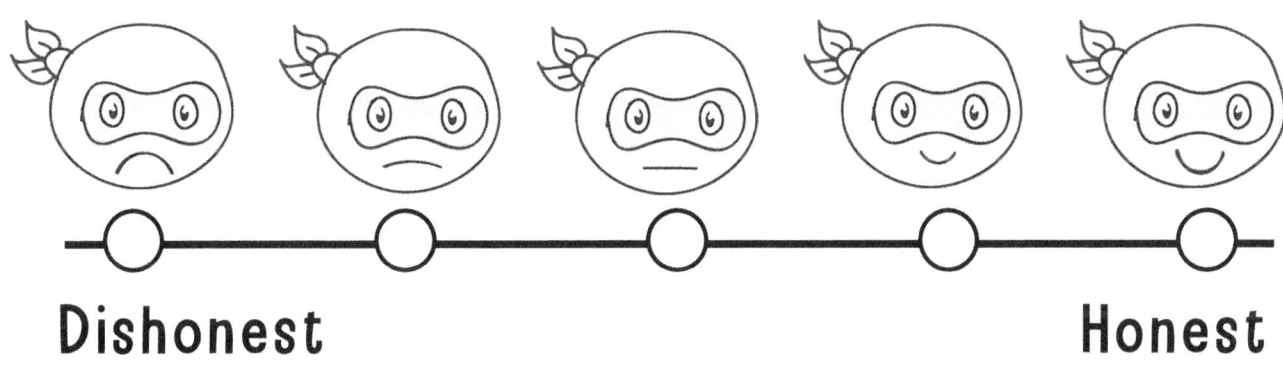

Dishonest   **Honest**

Growth Mindset

Chapter 10

Mistakes help your brain grow.

CHART

What else helps your brain grow?

Moving
What's your favorite sport?

Sleeping
What do you like doing right before bed?

Learning
What's a new thing you recently learned to do?

Eating
What's your favorite food?

Perfect Ninja must do things perfectly. When his own expectations aren't met, he becomes frustrated and ends up breaking down, crying, or giving up.

But everything changes one day when a friend shows him that mistakes and failures are the best teachers to help us learn and grow.

What I want to do	What others will think	What will I do about it

Money

Chapter 11

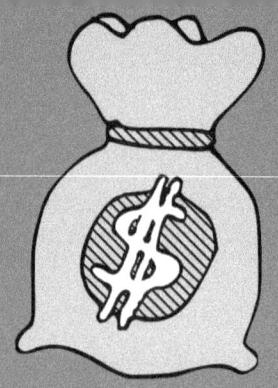

Some people are so **poor,** all they have is **money.**

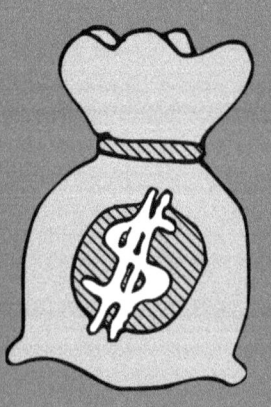

What are some things you would do if you had all the money in the world? List or draw them here.

Money Ninja said that money is not just to spend, but you can also save, invest, and donate. She saves her money in the bank and her piggy bank. She invests in several small businesses—her lemonade stand, candy machines, and a YouTube channel.

But of all the things she can do with money, her favorite way to use it is to donate it to charity because it makes her feel good.

Circle the things you value most:

Buying new stuff	Friendship	Clothes
Family	Nature	People
Knowledge	God	Laughter
Books	Earth	Trophies
Love	Shoes	Helping others

Do you have any business ideas?
List or draw them here:

Patience

Chapter 12

Patience is the **calm acceptance** that things can happen in a **different order** than the one you had in your mind.

Put an **X** where you fall on the patience scale and an **O** where you want to be.

Impatient   Patient

Patient Ninja used to be very impatient until she learned how to be more patient. One of her favorite tools to use is to:

Think through the consequences.

If I try to finish first, my work might end up sloppy and my spinner might not spin. I want to make the best possible spinner, so I need to work carefully.

What are some things you can be more patient about?
List or draw them here:

Diversity

Chapter 13

In diversity lies
beauty
and
strength.

Diversity Ninja shows us that regardless of differences in race, gender, ability, background, clothing, language spoken, or skin color, we are all part of the human race.

Do you know someone who is different? List or draw them here.

How are you and this person the same?

I am unique.

This is what makes me unique.
Make a list below.

Draw yourself below wearing a fun and unique outfit.

Courage

Chapter 14

Fear
is a reaction.
Courage
is a decision.

–Sir Winston Churchill

Brave Ninja was the bravest ninja in the world. But she wasn't always like this. She used to be scared to speak up or do things she wanted. So she practices the B-R-A-V-E method to become more courageous.

Breathe by taking a few deep breaths.

Relax your muscles.

Adopt positive body language.

Visualize your success.

Embrace a mantra.

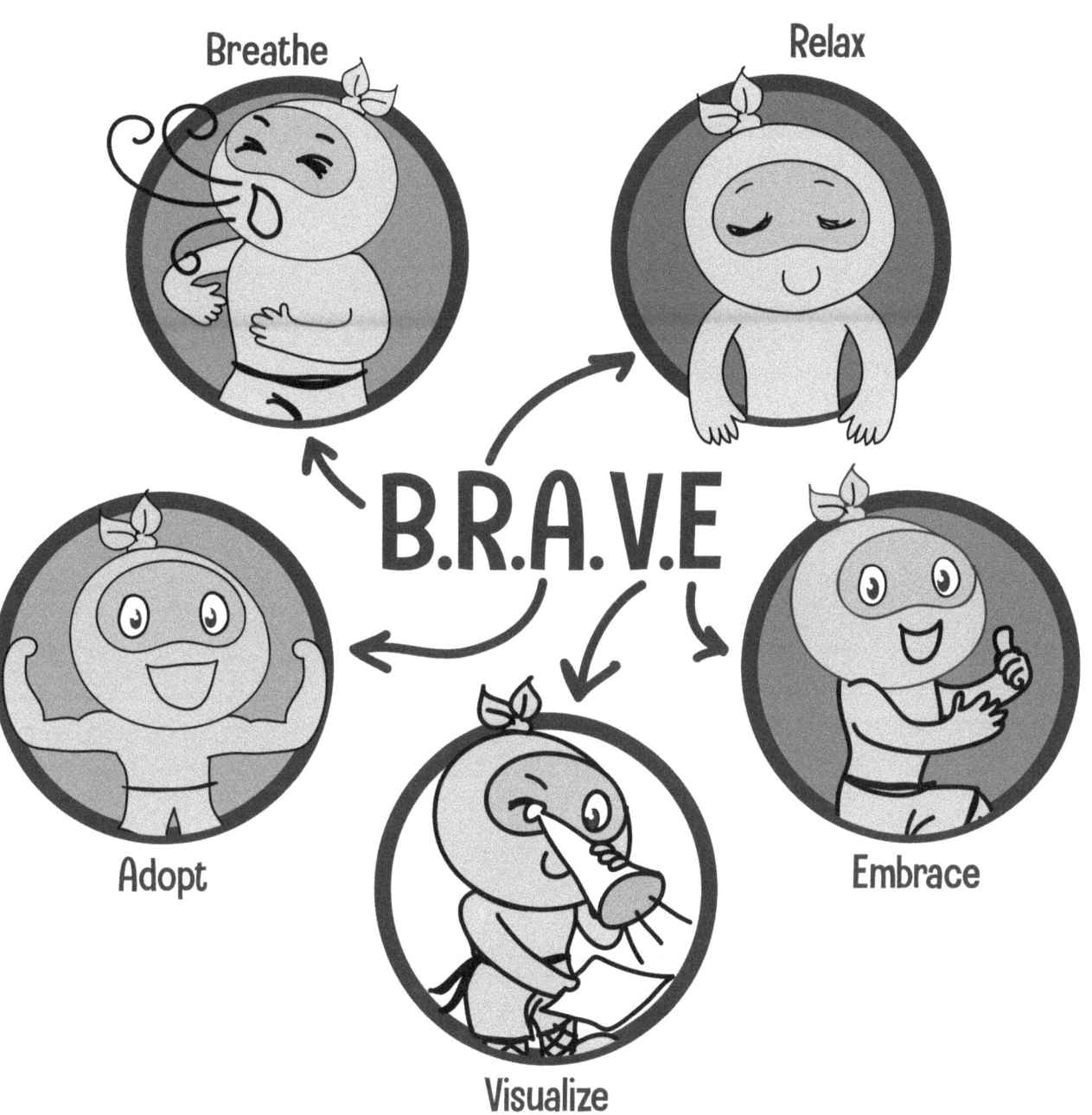

Organization

Chapter 15

Being organized can help your life by making it simpler.

Draw an **X** where your organizational skills are now and an **O** where you want to be.

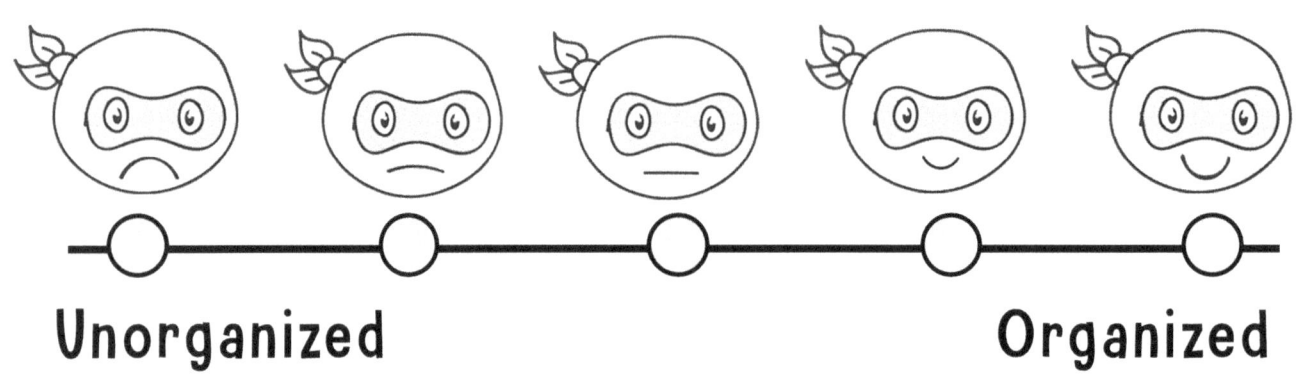

Unorganized   Organized

Organized Ninja used to be messy until he's introduced to the Cs:

Checklists
Collections
Categories

Do you collect anything? Draw or list it here.

Look around your home. Is anything categorized? List or draw it here.

Calm

Chapter 16

Your **calm** is your best weapon against ALL of your challenges.

Rate your calmness on this scale.

Not Calm   **Calm**

Calm Ninja Yoga Poses

Here's my downward dog.

I can slither like a cobra.

I am brave like a warrior.

I am strong like a boat.

I am as powerful as a lion.

Effort

Chapter 17

Our greatest

weakness

lies in giving up.

The most certain way to

succeed

is always to try just one

more time.

—Thomas Edison

Hard work beats talent when talent doesn't work hard.

What do you think this means?

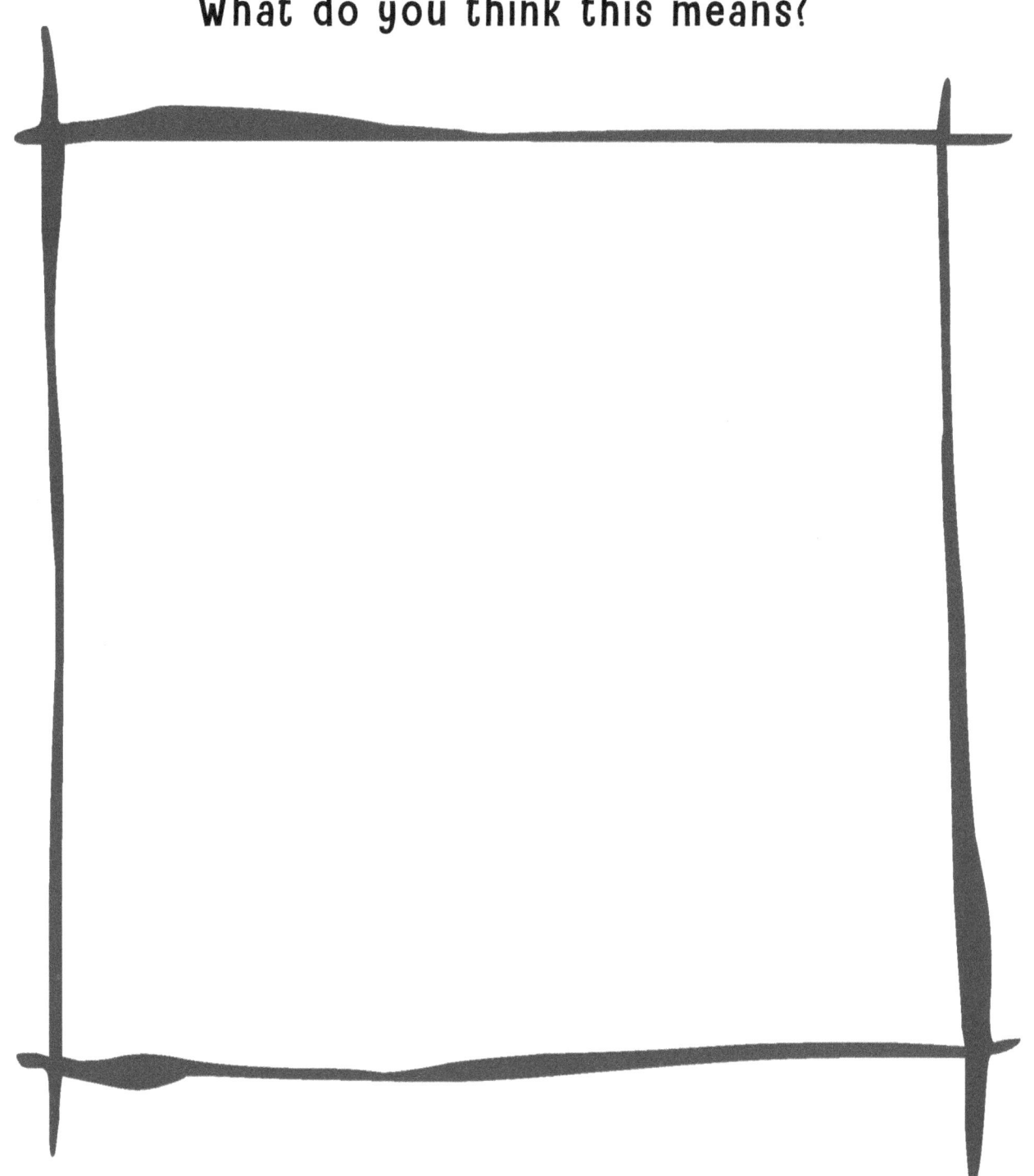

Smart Ninja excelled at many things. But when things became too hard, she got discouraged easily.

She learned a strategy that helped her overcome challenges. Do you know what the method is called? Write it down here. _____

_____

_____

_____

Think of a problem you are having. How can you handle it? How can you best approach it with a growth mindset?

Confidence

Chapter 18

No one can make you feel *INFERIOR* without your consent.

-Eleanor Roosevelt

Draw yourself on the mountain. Imagine what you could accomplish if you had no fear.

Confident Ninja learned how to achieve more confidence by practicing the Confidence Code.

The Confidence Code contains three parts:

Picture yourself succeeding.
Practice failing.
Put your goals down on paper.

Focus

Chapter 19

Focusing
is about
saying
No.

-Steve Jobs

We all need focus to achieve.
Where are you on the focus scale:

Unfocused — — — — — Focused

Focused Ninja shares that even if we aren't born with amazing focus (many of us aren't), we can learn to become more focused by using the F.O.C.U.S. method:

Find distractions and eliminate them.

Organize.

Choose greens and healthy foods.

Use exercise to give your brain a boost.

Split up large assignments into smaller tasks.

How do you stay organized?

How do you limit distractions?

What greens and healthy foods do you eat?

Which tasks do you divide up into smaller ones?

Inclusion

Chapter 20

Diversity
is being invited

to the party;

inclusion

is being asked to dance.

—Verna Myers

Practicing inclusion means you intentionally seek to include everyone, no matter their skin color, beliefs, religion, gender, clothing, language they speak, or background.

List or draw one way you've been inclusive.

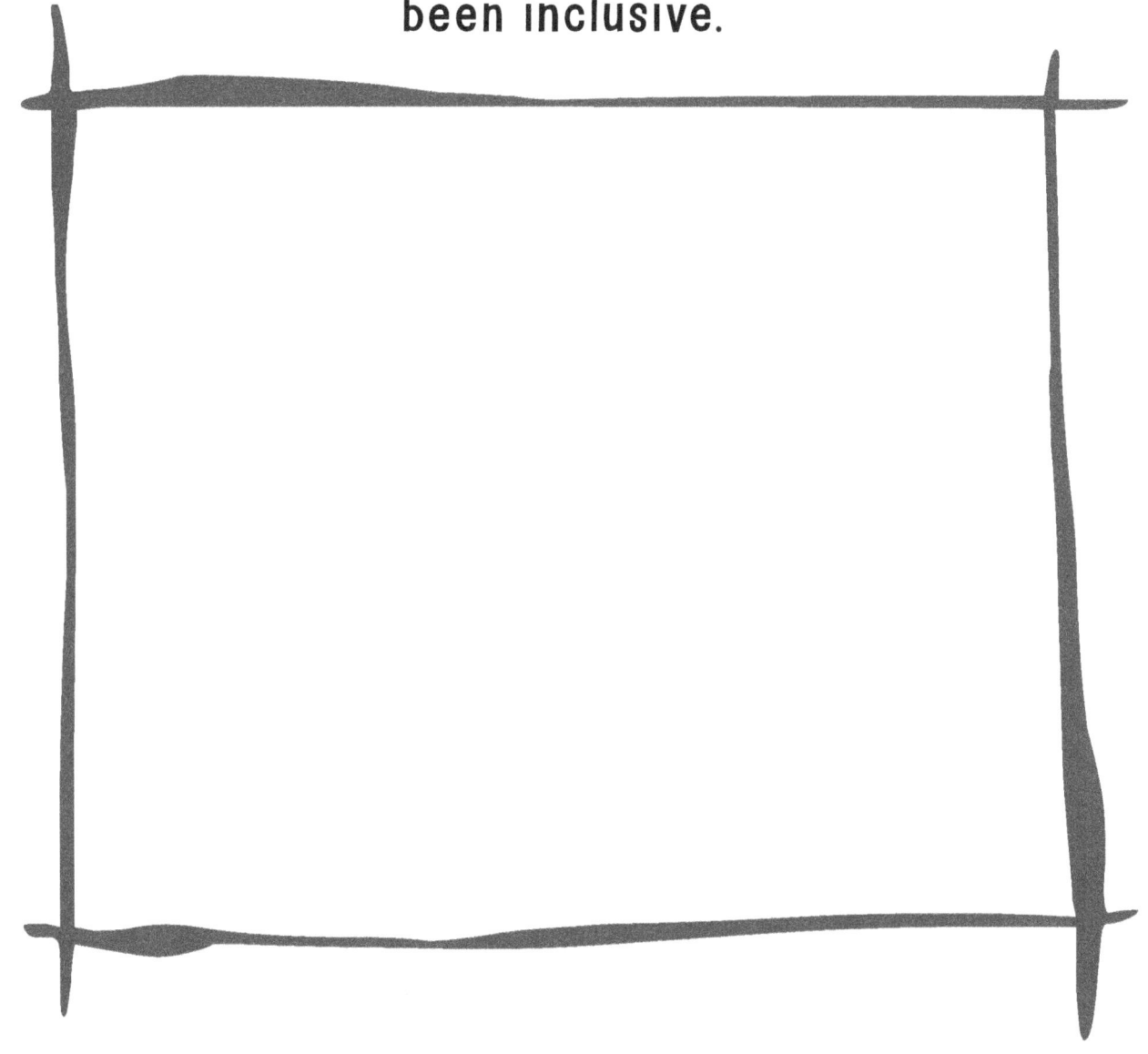

Developing compassion is the best way to practice inclusion. Compassion begins with putting ourselves in another person's shoes to see how they feel.

How do you feel when you are being compassionate?

Draw or list it here.

Communication

Chapter 21

Communication **works** for those who **work** at it.
—John Powell

Learning how to talk and listen are some of the most important life skills.

On a scale of 1 to 10, rate yourself
on your communication skills,
with 10 being the best.

1 2 3 4 5 6 7 8 9 10

On a scale of 1 to 10, rate yourself
on your listening skills,
with 10 being the best.

1 2 3 4 5 6 7 8 9 10

Communication Ninja used to struggle with communicating her emotions and feelings, but then she learned a strategy that helped her blossom into a wonderful communicator.

In the lines below, what method does Communication Ninja use to improve her communication skills?

_____

_____

_____

_____

Think of a time when you really, really listened when the other person was talking and you could you feel their emotions.

How did it make you feel?

Sad

Angry

Happy

Proud

Hope

Chapter 22

Once you CHOOSE hope, anything's possible.

—Christopher Reeves

Go outside at night and look up into the sky, up at the stars.

Make a wish and draw or write it down here:

Things I want to be	Why I want to be them

Humor

👍 Chapter 23

Humor
is mankind's
greatest
blessing.

–Mark Twain

Here are some funny jokes.

Why are teddy bears never hungry?
They're always stuffed!

What did the policeman say to his tummy?
Freeze. You're under a vest.

What does one volcano say to the other?
I lava you!

What do kids play when they can't play with a phone?
Bored games.

What game does the sky love to play?
Twister.

Why do we never tell jokes about pizza?
They're too cheesy.

Did you hear the joke about the roof?
Never mind, it's over your head.

What time is it when people are throwing pieces of bread at your head?
Time to duck.

What's the difference between a guitar and a fish?
You can tune a guitar, but you can't tuna fish.

What did the sink say to the potty?
You look flushed!

What's a snake's strongest subject in school?
Hiss-tory.

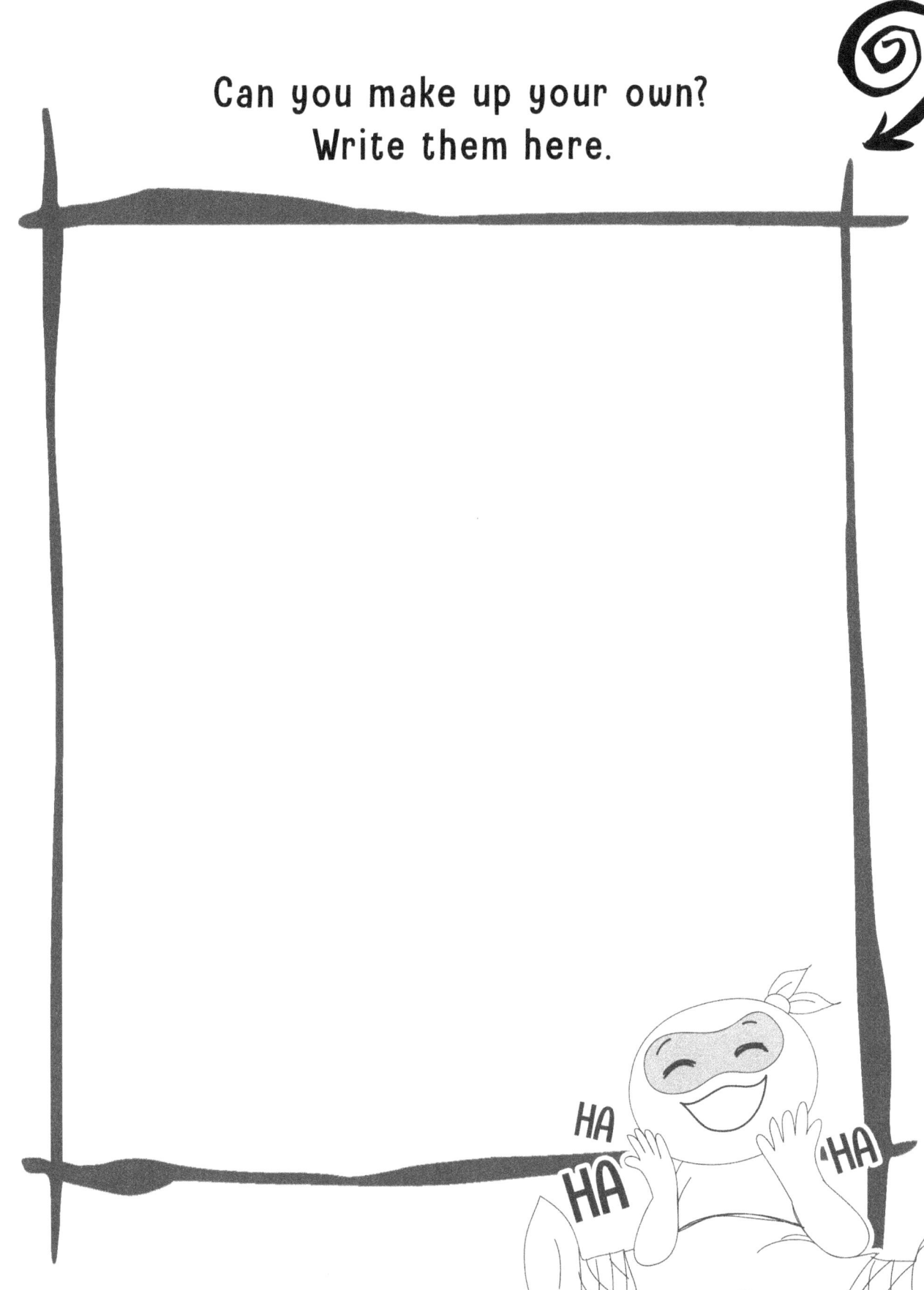

Can you make up your own?
Write them here.

Think of a funny moment in your life. Draw a comic strip about it.

"Why was 6 afraid of 7?" asked Inclusive Ninja.

"I dont know," replied Diversity NInja.

"Because 7, 8, 9," said Inclusive Ninja and they both laughed hysterically.

Self- belief coloring pages

I believe in myself!

When the going gets tough, I get tougher.

I can be anything I want to be.

I am PATIENT.

I am GRITTY.

I am honest.

Visit us at NinjaLifeHacks.tv for more fun resources.

@marynhin @officialninjalifehacks
#NinjaLifeHacks

Mary Nhin   Ninja Life Hacks

Ninja Life Hacks

@officialninjalifehacks

www.ingramcontent.com/pod-product-compliance
Lightning Source LLC
Chambersburg PA
CBHW042358070526
44585CB00029B/2974